This book belongs to:

_____

To my little bears
Scottie and Owen

Every morning,
Scottie woke in his big blue house...

and changed out of his PJs
ready to go out.
He went to school
or to the mall...

... PARADES were his favorite of them all.

One day Mummy said,
"We're moving to a new city,
With a new school,
new teacher and new kiddies!"

Slowly things got packed away...

...and a BIG TRUCK came to pick them up one day!

"Have a good night," said Mummy, "Tomorrow we fly to somewhere warm and sunny."

Goodbye house,
goodbye trees, goodbye friends,
When we come back to visit
we'll play again

Goodbye teacher and classroom too,

goodbye animals at the zoo.

Scottie was excited for the big plane ride.
He ate snacks, did mazes and looked outside.
He helped Mummy and Daddy make baby Owen giggle.
"You have to be gentle," he said, "because he's little."

When the plane landed they got into a car.
"It's been a long day," he said, "we've travelled far."
When they arrived to their new home,
Scottie saw a big truck
and a new yard to roam.

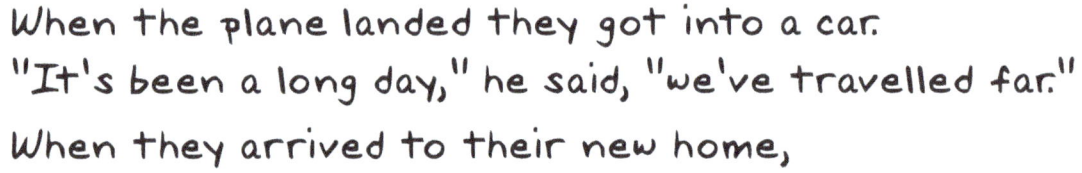

He was so tired...
what's that on his bed?
It's Bear and Monkey!
And a pillow for his head.

On the first day of school,
Scottie was a bit nervous
But the kids were friendly
and said, "Come play with us!"

Everything was a bit different
but Scottie did well

When Mummy came to pick him up he had lots to tell.

Things can be a bit scary
when everything is new.
It helped Scottie to have things he knew.
He knew Mummy, Daddy and Owen were always there
And of course, there's always Monkey and Bear.

Day by day, things got better
Best of all was the weather.

Hello sunshine,
 hello pool, hello trees,
Hello leaves
 whispering in the breeze.

Now Scottie wakes
in his big brick house
And changes out of his PJs
ready to go out.
He goes to school or the mall...

...BIKE RIDES are his favorite of them all.

NEW NEIGHBORHOOD CHECKLIST

- [ ] Find the closest playground
- [ ] Say hi to a new neighbor
- [ ] Which neighbor is closest to your age?
- [ ] Share a toy with a new friend
- [ ] Get mail from the new mailbox
- [ ] Help unpack one box
- [ ] Find the closest ice cream store
- [ ] Run around in a park
- [ ] Find the moon in the sky
- [ ] Try one new food

www.ingramcontent.com/pod-product-compliance
Lightning Source LLC
Chambersburg PA
CBHW080456240426
43673CB00005B/208

Welcome guests

...and enter with a happy heart!
May all who enter as guests, leave as friends!

Guest name:

Dates of stay:

Visiting from:

Message to host:

Favorite moments (special highlights of your stay):

Recommendations for future guests (such as restaurants, entertainment, sites to see, etc.):

Guest name:

Dates of stay:

Visiting from:

Message to host :

Favorite moments (special highlights of your stay):

Recommendations for future guests (such as restaurants, entertainment, sites to see, etc.):

Guest name:

Dates of stay:

Visiting from:

Message to host:

Favorite moments (special highlights of your stay):

Recommendations for future guests (such as restaurants, entertainment, sites to see, etc.):

Guest name:

Dates of stay:

Visiting from:

Message to host:

Favorite moments (special highlights of your stay):

Recommendations for future guests (such as restaurants, entertainment, sites to see, etc.):

Guest name:

Dates of stay:

Visiting from:

Message to host:

Favorite moments (special highlights of your stay):

Recommendations for future guests (such as restaurants, entertainment, sites to see, etc.):

Guest name:

Dates of stay:

Visiting from:

Message to host :

Favorite moments (special highlights of your stay):

Recommendations for future guests (such as restaurants, entertainment, sites to see, etc.):

Guest name:

Dates of stay:

Visiting from:

Message to host:

Favorite moments (special highlights of your stay):

Recommendations for future guests (such as restaurants, entertainment, sites to see, etc.):

Guest name:

Dates of stay:

Visiting from:

Message to host:

Favorite moments (special highlights of your stay):

Recommendations for future guests (such as restaurants, entertainment, sites to see, etc.):

Guest name:

Dates of stay:

Visiting from:

Message to host:

Favorite moments (special highlights of your stay):

Recommendations for future guests (such as restaurants, entertainment, sites to see, etc.):

Guest name:

Dates of stay:

Visiting from:

Message to host:

Favorite moments (special highlights of your stay):

Recommendations for future guests (such as restaurants, entertainment, sites to see, etc.):

Guest name:

Dates of stay:

Visiting from:

Message to host:

Favorite moments (special highlights of your stay):

Recommendations for future guests (such as restaurants, entertainment, sites to see, etc.):

Guest name:

Dates of stay:

Visiting from:

Message to host :

Favorite moments (special highlights of your stay):

Recommendations for future guests (such as restaurants, entertainment, sites to see, etc.):

Guest name:

Dates of stay:

Visiting from:

Message to host:

Favorite moments (special highlights of your stay):

Recommendations for future guests (such as restaurants, entertainment, sites to see, etc.):

Guest name:

Dates of stay:

Visiting from:

Message to host :

Favorite moments (special highlights of your stay):

Recommendations for future guests (such as restaurants, entertainment, sites to see, etc.):

Guest name:

Dates of stay:

Visiting from:

Message to host :

Favorite moments (special highlights of your stay):

Recommendations for future guests (such as restaurants, entertainment, sites to see, etc.):

Guest name:

Dates of stay:

Visiting from:

Message to host:

Favorite moments (special highlights of your stay):

Recommendations for future guests (such as restaurants, entertainment, sites to see, etc.):

Guest name:

Dates of stay:

Visiting from:

Message to host:

Favorite moments (special highlights of your stay):

Recommendations for future guests (such as restaurants, entertainment, sites to see, etc.):

Guest name:

Dates of stay:

Visiting from:

Message to host:

Favorite moments (special highlights of your stay):

Recommendations for future guests (such as restaurants, entertainment, sites to see, etc.):

Guest name:

Dates of stay:

Visiting from:

Message to host :

Favorite moments (special highlights of your stay):

Recommendations for future guests (such as restaurants, entertainment, sites to see, etc.):

Guest name:

Dates of stay:

Visiting from:

Message to host :

Favorite moments (special highlights of your stay):

Recommendations for future guests (such as restaurants, entertainment, sites to see, etc.):

Guest name:

Dates of stay:

Visiting from:

Message to host:

Favorite moments (special highlights of your stay):

Recommendations for future guests (such as restaurants, entertainment, sites to see, etc.):

Guest name:

Dates of stay:

Visiting from:

Message to host :

Favorite moments (special highlights of your stay):

Recommendations for future guests (such as restaurants, entertainment, sites to see, etc.):

Guest name:

Dates of stay:

Visiting from:

Message to host:

Favorite moments (special highlights of your stay):

Recommendations for future guests (such as restaurants, entertainment, sites to see, etc.):

Guest name:

Dates of stay:

Visiting from:

Message to host:

Favorite moments (special highlights of your stay):

Recommendations for future guests (such as restaurants, entertainment, sites to see, etc.):

Guest name:

Dates of stay:

Visiting from:

Message to host :

Favorite moments (special highlights of your stay):

Recommendations for future guests (such as restaurants, entertainment, sites to see, etc.):

Guest name:

Dates of stay:

Visiting from:

Message to host:

Favorite moments (special highlights of your stay):

Recommendations for future guests (such as restaurants, entertainment, sites to see, etc.):

Guest name:

Dates of stay:

Visiting from:

Message to host:

Favorite moments (special highlights of your stay):

Recommendations for future guests (such as restaurants, entertainment, sites to see, etc.):

Guest name:

Dates of stay:

Visiting from:

Message to host:

Favorite moments (special highlights of your stay):

Recommendations for future guests (such as restaurants, entertainment, sites to see, etc.):

Guest name:

Dates of stay:

Visiting from:

Message to host:

Favorite moments (special highlights of your stay):

Recommendations for future guests (such as restaurants, entertainment, sites to see, etc.):

Guest name:

Dates of stay:

Visiting from:

Message to host:

Favorite moments (special highlights of your stay):

Recommendations for future guests (such as restaurants, entertainment, sites to see, etc.):

Guest name:

Dates of stay:

Visiting from:

Message to host:

Favorite moments (special highlights of your stay):

Recommendations for future guests (such as restaurants, entertainment, sites to see, etc.):

Guest name:

Dates of stay:

Visiting from:

Message to host :

Favorite moments (special highlights of your stay):

Recommendations for future guests (such as restaurants, entertainment, sites to see, etc.):

Guest name:

Dates of stay:

Visiting from:

Message to host :

Favorite moments (special highlights of your stay):

Recommendations for future guests (such as restaurants, entertainment, sites to see, etc.):

Guest name:

Dates of stay:

Visiting from:

Message to host:

Favorite moments (special highlights of your stay):

Recommendations for future guests (such as restaurants, entertainment, sites to see, etc.):

Guest name:

Dates of stay:

Visiting from:

Message to host :

Favorite moments (special highlights of your stay):

Recommendations for future guests (such as restaurants, entertainment, sites to see, etc.).

Guest name:

Dates of stay:

Visiting from:

Message to host :

Favorite moments (special highlights of your stay):

Recommendations for future guests (such as restaurants, entertainment, sites to see, etc.):

Guest name:

Dates of stay:

Visiting from:

Message to host :

Favorite moments (special highlights of your stay):

Recommendations for future guests (such as restaurants, entertainment, sites to see, etc.):

Guest name:

Dates of stay:

Visiting from:

Message to host:

Favorite moments (special highlights of your stay):

Recommendations for future guests (such as restaurants, entertainment, sites to see, etc.):

Guest name:

Dates of stay:

Visiting from:

Message to host:

Favorite moments (special highlights of your stay):

Recommendations for future guests (such as restaurants, entertainment, sites to see, etc.):

Guest name:

Dates of stay:

Visiting from:

Message to host:

Favorite moments (special highlights of your stay):

Recommendations for future guests (such as restaurants, entertainment, sites to see, etc.):

Guest name:

Dates of stay:

Visiting from:

Message to host:

Favorite moments (special highlights of your stay):

Recommendations for future guests (such as restaurants, entertainment, sites to see, etc.):

Guest name:

Dates of stay:

Visiting from:

Message to host:

Favorite moments (special highlights of your stay):

Recommendations for future guests (such as restaurants, entertainment, sites to see, etc.):

Guest name:

Dates of stay:

Visiting from:

Message to host :

Favorite moments (special highlights of your stay):

Recommendations for future guests (such as restaurants, entertainment, sites to see, etc.):

Guest name:

Dates of stay:

Visiting from:

Message to host :

Favorite moments (special highlights of your stay):

Recommendations for future guests (such as restaurants, entertainment, sites to see, etc.):

Guest name:

Dates of stay:

Visiting from:

Message to host :

Favorite moments (special highlights of your stay):

Recommendations for future guests (such as restaurants, entertainment, sites to see, etc.):

Guest name:

Dates of stay:

Visiting from:

Message to host:

Favorite moments (special highlights of your stay):

Recommendations for future guests (such as restaurants, entertainment, sites to see, etc.):

Guest name:

Dates of stay:

Visiting from:

Message to host:

Favorite moments (special highlights of your stay):

Recommendations for future guests (such as restaurants, entertainment, sites to see, etc.):

Guest name:

Dates of stay:

Visiting from:

Message to host:

Favorite moments (special highlights of your stay):

Recommendations for future guests (such as restaurants, entertainment, sites to see, etc.):

Guest name:

Dates of stay:

Visiting from:

Message to host:

Favorite moments (special highlights of your stay):

Recommendations for future guests (such as restaurants, entertainment, sites to see, etc.):

Guest name:

Dates of stay:

Visiting from:

Message to host :

Favorite moments (special highlights of your stay):

Recommendations for future guests (such as restaurants, entertainment, sites to see, etc.):

Guest name:

Dates of stay:

Visiting from:

Message to host:

Favorite moments (special highlights of your stay):

Recommendations for future guests (such as restaurants, entertainment, sites to see, etc.):

Guest name:

Dates of stay:

Visiting from:

Message to host :

Favorite moments (special highlights of your stay):

Recommendations for future guests (such as restaurants, entertainment, sites to see, etc.):

Guest name:

Dates of stay:

Visiting from:

Message to host:

Favorite moments (special highlights of your stay):

Recommendations for future guests (such as restaurants, entertainment, sites to see, etc.):

Guest name:

Dates of stay:

Visiting from:

Message to host :

Favorite moments (special highlights of your stay):

Recommendations for future guests (such as restaurants, entertainment, sites to see, etc.):

Guest name:

Dates of stay:

Visiting from:

Message to host:

Favorite moments (special highlights of your stay):

Recommendations for future guests (such as restaurants, entertainment, sites to see, etc.):

Guest name:

Dates of stay:

Visiting from:

Message to host:

Favorite moments (special highlights of your stay):

Recommendations for future guests (such as restaurants, entertainment, sites to see, etc.):

Guest name:

Dates of stay:

Visiting from:

Message to host :

Favorite moments (special highlights of your stay):

Recommendations for future guests (such as restaurants, entertainment, sites to see, etc.):

Guest name:

Dates of stay:

Visiting from:

Message to host:

Favorite moments (special highlights of your stay):

Recommendations for future guests (such as restaurants, entertainment, sites to see, etc.):

Guest name:

Dates of stay:

Visiting from:

Message to host :

Favorite moments (special highlights of your stay):

Recommendations for future guests (such as restaurants, entertainment, sites to see, etc.):

Guest name:

Dates of stay:

Visiting from:

Message to host:

Favorite moments (special highlights of your stay):

Recommendations for future guests (such as restaurants, entertainment, sites to see, etc.):

Guest name:

Dates of stay:

Visiting from:

Message to host :

Favorite moments (special highlights of your stay):

Recommendations for future guests (such as restaurants, entertainment, sites to see, etc.):

Guest name:

Dates of stay:

Visiting from:

Message to host:

Favorite moments (special highlights of your stay):

Recommendations for future guests (such as restaurants, entertainment, sites to see, etc.):

Guest name:

Dates of stay:

Visiting from:

Message to host:

Favorite moments (special highlights of your stay):

Recommendations for future guests (such as restaurants, entertainment, sites to see, etc.):

Guest name:

Dates of stay:

Visiting from:

Message to host:

Favorite moments (special highlights of your stay):

Recommendations for future guests (such as restaurants, entertainment, sites to see, etc.):

Guest name:

Dates of stay:

Visiting from:

Message to host:

Favorite moments (special highlights of your stay):

Recommendations for future guests (such as restaurants, entertainment, sites to see, etc.):

Guest name:

Dates of stay:

Visiting from:

Message to host:

Favorite moments (special highlights of your stay):

Recommendations for future guests (such as restaurants, entertainment, sites to see, etc.):

Guest name:

Dates of stay:

Visiting from:

Message to host:

Favorite moments (special highlights of your stay):

Recommendations for future guests (such as restaurants, entertainment, sites to see, etc.):

Guest name:

Dates of stay:

Visiting from:

Message to host:

Favorite moments (special highlights of your stay):

Recommendations for future guests (such as restaurants, entertainment, sites to see, etc.):

Guest name:

Dates of stay:

Visiting from:

Message to host:

Favorite moments (special highlights of your stay):

Recommendations for future guests (such as restaurants, entertainment, sites to see, etc.):

Guest name:

Dates of stay:

Visiting from:

Message to host :

Favorite moments (special highlights of your stay):

Recommendations for future guests (such as restaurants, entertainment, sites to see, etc.):

Guest name:

Dates of stay:

Visiting from:

Message to host:

Favorite moments (special highlights of your stay):

Recommendations for future guests (such as restaurants, entertainment, sites to see, etc.):

Guest name:

Dates of stay:

Visiting from:

Message to host:

Favorite moments (special highlights of your stay):

Recommendations for future guests (such as restaurants, entertainment, sites to see, etc.):

Guest name:

Dates of stay:

Visiting from:

Message to host:

Favorite moments (special highlights of your stay):

Recommendations for future guests (such as restaurants, entertainment, sites to see, etc.):

Guest name:

Dates of stay:

Visiting from:

Message to host :

Favorite moments (special highlights of your stay):

Recommendations for future guests (such as restaurants, entertainment, sites to see, etc.):

Guest name:

Dates of stay:

Visiting from:

Message to host:

Favorite moments (special highlights of your stay):

Recommendations for future guests (such as restaurants, entertainment, sites to see, etc.):

Guest name:

Dates of stay:

Visiting from:

Message to host:

Favorite moments (special highlights of your stay):

Recommendations for future guests (such as restaurants, entertainment, sites to see, etc.):

Guest name:

Dates of stay:

Visiting from:

Message to host:

Favorite moments (special highlights of your stay):

Recommendations for future guests (such as restaurants, entertainment, sites to see, etc.):

Guest name:

Dates of stay:

Visiting from:

Message to host :

Favorite moments (special highlights of your stay):

Recommendations for future guests (such as restaurants, entertainment, sites to see, etc.):

Guest name:

Dates of stay:

Visiting from:

Message to host :

Favorite moments (special highlights of your stay):

Recommendations for future guests (such as restaurants, entertainment, sites to see, etc.):

Guest name:

Dates of stay:

Visiting from:

Message to host:

Favorite moments (special highlights of your stay):

Recommendations for future guests (such as restaurants, entertainment, sites to see, etc.):

Guest name:

Dates of stay:

Visiting from:

Message to host :

Favorite moments (special highlights of your stay):

Recommendations for future guests (such as restaurants, entertainment, sites to see, etc.):

Guest name:

Dates of stay:

Visiting from:

Message to host :

Favorite moments (special highlights of your stay):

Recommendations for future guests (such as restaurants, entertainment, sites to see, etc.):

Guest name:

Dates of stay:

Visiting from:

Message to host:

Favorite moments (special highlights of your stay):

Recommendations for future guests (such as restaurants, entertainment, sites to see, etc.):

Guest name:

Dates of stay:

Visiting from:

Message to host:

Favorite moments (special highlights of your stay):

Recommendations for future guests (such as restaurants, entertainment, sites to see, etc.):

Guest name:

Dates of stay:

Visiting from:

Message to host :

Favorite moments (special highlights of your stay):

Recommendations for future guests (such as restaurants, entertainment, sites to see, etc.):

Guest name:

Dates of stay:

Visiting from:

Message to host:

Favorite moments (special highlights of your stay):

Recommendations for future guests (such as restaurants, entertainment, sites to see, etc.):

Guest name:

Dates of stay:

Visiting from:

Message to host :

Favorite moments (special highlights of your stay):

Recommendations for future guests (such as restaurants, entertainment, sites to see, etc.):

Guest name:

Dates of stay:

Visiting from:

Message to host :

Favorite moments (special highlights of your stay):

Recommendations for future guests (such as restaurants, entertainment, sites to see, etc.):

Guest name:

Dates of stay:

Visiting from:

Message to host:

Favorite moments (special highlights of your stay):

Recommendations for future guests (such as restaurants, entertainment, sites to see, etc.):

Guest name:

Dates of stay:

Visiting from:

Message to host:

Favorite moments (special highlights of your stay):

Recommendations for future guests (such as restaurants, entertainment, sites to see, etc.):

Guest name:

Dates of stay:

Visiting from:

Message to host:

Favorite moments (special highlights of your stay):

Recommendations for future guests (such as restaurants, entertainment, sites to see, etc.):

Guest name:

Dates of stay:

Visiting from:

Message to host :

Favorite moments (special highlights of your stay):

Recommendations for future guests (such as restaurants, entertainment, sites to see, etc.):

Guest name:

Dates of stay:

Visiting from:

Message to host:

Favorite moments (special highlights of your stay):

Recommendations for future guests (such as restaurants, entertainment, sites to see, etc.):

Guest name:

Dates of stay:

Visiting from:

Message to host:

Favorite moments (special highlights of your stay):

Recommendations for future guests (such as restaurants, entertainment, sites to see, etc.):

Guest name:

Dates of stay:

Visiting from:

Message to host:

Favorite moments (special highlights of your stay):

Recommendations for future guests (such as restaurants, entertainment, sites to see, etc.):

Guest name:

Dates of stay:

Visiting from:

Message to host :

Favorite moments (special highlights of your stay):

Recommendations for future guests (such as restaurants, entertainment, sites to see, etc.):

Guest name:

Dates of stay:

Visiting from:

Message to host :

Favorite moments (special highlights of your stay):

Recommendations for future guests (such as restaurants, entertainment, sites to see, etc.):

Guest name:

Dates of stay:

Visiting from:

Message to host:

Favorite moments (special highlights of your stay):

Recommendations for future guests (such as restaurants, entertainment, sites to see, etc.):

Guest name:

Dates of stay:

Visiting from:

Message to host :

Favorite moments (special highlights of your stay):

Recommendations for future guests (such as restaurants, entertainment, sites to see, etc.):

Guest name:

Dates of stay:

Visiting from:

Message to host :

Favorite moments (special highlights of your stay):

Recommendations for future guests (such as restaurants, entertainment, sites to see, etc.):

Guest name:

Dates of stay:

Visiting from:

Message to host :

Favorite moments (special highlights of your stay):

Recommendations for future guests (such as restaurants, entertainment, sites to see, etc.):

Guest name:

Dates of stay:

Visiting from:

Message to host :

Favorite moments (special highlights of your stay):

Recommendations for future guests (such as restaurants, entertainment, sites to see, etc.):

Guest name:

Dates of stay:

Visiting from:

Message to host:

Favorite moments (special highlights of your stay):

Recommendations for future guests (such as restaurants, entertainment, sites to see, etc.):

Guest name:

Dates of stay:

Visiting from:

Message to host:

Favorite moments (special highlights of your stay):

Recommendations for future guests (such as restaurants, entertainment, sites to see, etc.):

Guest name:

Dates of stay:

Visiting from:

Message to host:

Favorite moments (special highlights of your stay):

Recommendations for future guests (such as restaurants, entertainment, sites to see, etc.):

Guest name:

Dates of stay:

Visiting from:

Message to host:

Favorite moments (special highlights of your stay):

Recommendations for future guests (such as restaurants, entertainment, sites to see, etc.):

Guest name:

Dates of stay:

Visiting from:

Message to host:

Favorite moments (special highlights of your stay):

Recommendations for future guests (such as restaurants, entertainment, sites to see, etc.):

Guest name:

Dates of stay:

Visiting from:

Message to host:

Favorite moments (special highlights of your stay):

Recommendations for future guests (such as restaurants, entertainment, sites to see, etc.):

Guest name:

Dates of stay:

Visiting from:

Message to host :

Favorite moments (special highlights of your stay):

Recommendations for future guests (such as restaurants, entertainment, sites to see, etc.):

Guest name:

Dates of stay:

Visiting from:

Message to host:

Favorite moments (special highlights of your stay):

Recommendations for future guests (such as restaurants, entertainment, sites to see, etc.):

Guest name:

Dates of stay:

Visiting from:

Message to host:

Favorite moments (special highlights of your stay):

Recommendations for future guests (such as restaurants, entertainment, sites to see, etc.):

Guest name:

Dates of stay:

Visiting from:

Message to host :

Favorite moments (special highlights of your stay):

Recommendations for future guests (such as restaurants, entertainment, sites to see, etc.):

Guest name:

Dates of stay:

Visiting from:

Message to host:

Favorite moments (special highlights of your stay):

Recommendations for future guests (such as restaurants, entertainment, sites to see, etc.):

Guest name:

Dates of stay:

Visiting from:

Message to host :

Favorite moments (special highlights of your stay):

Recommendations for future guests (such as restaurants, entertainment, sites to see, etc.):

Guest name:

Dates of stay:

Visiting from:

Message to host:

Favorite moments (special highlights of your stay):

Recommendations for future guests (such as restaurants, entertainment, sites to see, etc.):

Guest name:

Dates of stay:

Visiting from:

Message to host:

Favorite moments (special highlights of your stay):

Recommendations for future guests (such as restaurants, entertainment, sites to see, etc.):

Guest name:

Dates of stay:

Visiting from:

Message to host:

Favorite moments (special highlights of your stay):

Recommendations for future guests (such as restaurants, entertainment, sites to see, etc.):

Guest name:

Dates of stay:

Visiting from:

Message to host:

Favorite moments (special highlights of your stay):

Recommendations for future guests (such as restaurants, entertainment, sites to see, etc.):

Guest name:

Dates of stay:

Visiting from:

Message to host:

Favorite moments (special highlights of your stay):

Recommendations for future guests (such as restaurants, entertainment, sites to see, etc.):

Guest name:

Dates of stay:

Visiting from:

Message to host :

Favorite moments (special highlights of your stay):

Recommendations for future guests (such as restaurants, entertainment, sites to see, etc.):

Thank you!

As a small family company, your feedback is very important to us.
Please let us know how you like our book at:

- **f** /createpublication
- 📷 /createpublication
- ✉ createpublication@gmail.com

Copyrights 2021 - All rights reserved

You may not reproduce, duplicate, or send the contents of this book without direct written permission from the author. You cannot hereby despite any circumstance blame the publisher or hold him or her the legal responsibility for any reparation, compensation or monetary forfeiture owing to the information included herein, either in a direct or indirect way.

Legal Notice: This book has copyright protection. You can use the book for personal purpose. You should not sell, use, alter, distribute, quote, take excerpts or paraphrase in part of whole the material contained in this book without obtaining the permission of the author first.

Disclaimer Notice: You must take note that the information in this document is for casual reading and entertainment purpose only. We have made every attempt to provide accurate, up to date and reliable information. We do not express or imply guarantees of any kind. The person who read admit that the writer is not occupied in giving legal, financial, medical, or other advice. We put this book content by sourcing various places.

Please consult a licensed professional before you try any techniques shown in this book.By going through this document, the book lover comes to an agreement that under no situation is the author accountable for any forfeiture, direct or indirect, which they may incur because of the use of material contained in this document, including, but not limited to, - errors, omissions, or inaccuracies.

www.ingramcontent.com/pod-product-compliance
Lightning Source LLC
Chambersburg PA
CBHW080456240426
43673CB00005B/209